Dear Family,

What's the best way to help your child love reading?

Find good books like this one to share—and read together!

Here are some tips.

●**Take a "pic**
at all the pictu

●**Take turns.**
voices for diffe
listen as your
her own word

●**Point out w**
letters and sou
words that yo
and what they

●**Ask questi**
example: "What do you think will happen next?" "How would you feel if that happened to you?"

●**Read every day.** Good stories are worth reading more than once! Read signs, labels, and even cereal boxes with your child. Visit the library to take out more books. And look for other JUST FOR YOU! BOOKS you and your child can share!

The Editor

5-05
3.99

For Olivia's cousins—Ethan, Alexa, and Jordan;
with special thanks to Cousin Cindy.
—BF
For illustrator Leonard Jenkins:
Thank you for the words of wisdom and the lessons in life; especially
for telling me, "Never put all your *apples* in one basket."
—GG

Library of Congress Cataloging-in-Publication Data

Ford, Bernette G.
    Don't hit me! / by Bernette Ford ; illustrated by Gary Grier.
       p. cm.—(Just for you! Level 1)
    Summary: When best friends get mad over a game of chess, one strikes out and
the other reminds him that they should use their words, not their fists, when they
disagree. Includes activity ideas for parents and children.
    ISBN 0-439-56860-9 (pbk.)
    [1. Conflict management—Fiction. 2. Behavior—Fiction. 3. Best friends—Fiction.
4. Friendship—Fiction. 5. African Americans—Fiction. 6. Stories in rhyme.]
    I. Title: Do not hit me!. II. Grier, Gary, ill. III. Title. IV. Series.

PZ8.3.F74Do 2004
[E]—dc22

2004042916

10 9 8 7   05 06 07 08
Printed in the U.S.A. 23 • First Scholastic Printing, February 2004

Don't Hit Me!

by Bernette Ford
Illustrated by Gary Grier

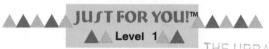

JUST FOR YOU!™
Level 1

You hit me!
Don't hit me!
You made me feel bad.

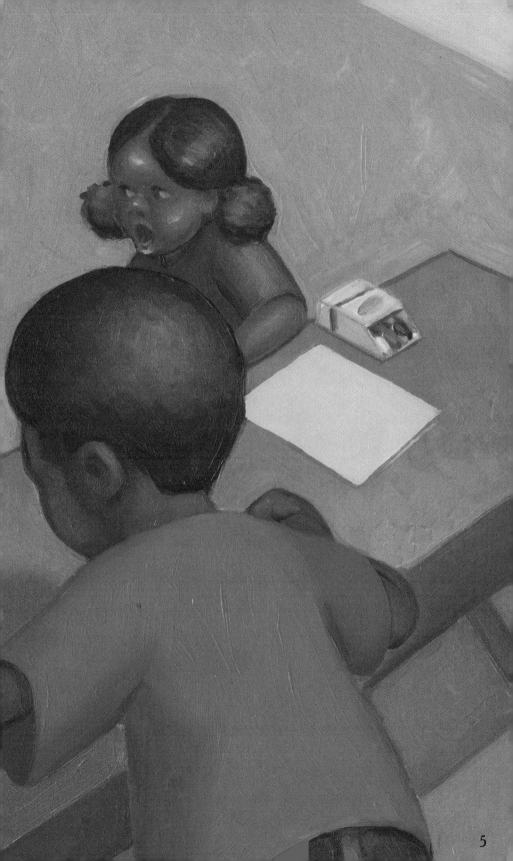

I know what I did
must have made you real mad.

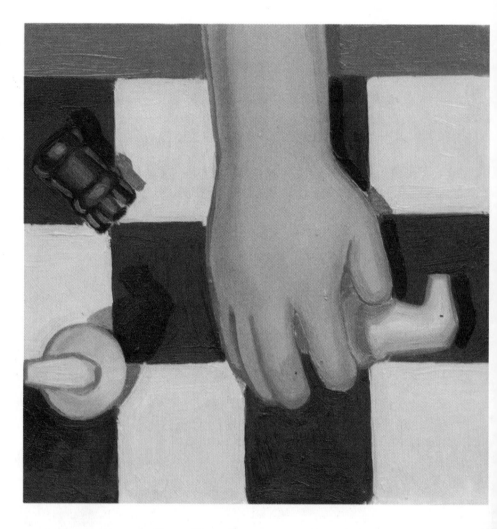

I took all your men.
I knocked down our game.

But you hit me so hard
I might call you a name!

I feel so bad that
I might start to cry.

I want to hit you right back—
I can't lie!

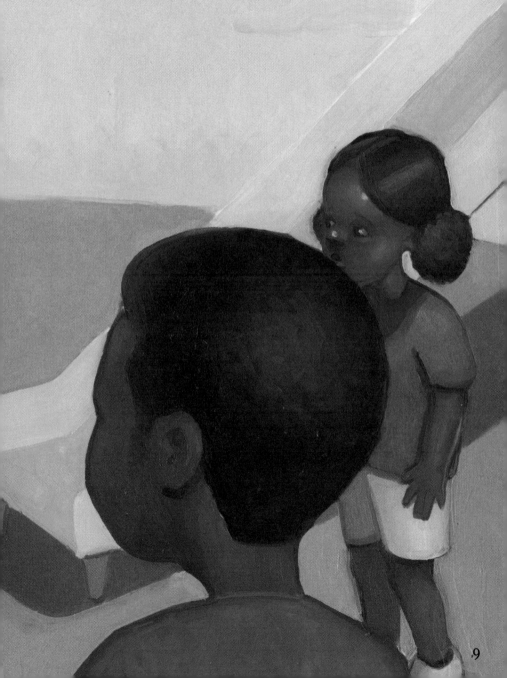

"Use your words!" says Miss Brown.
"Use your words, not your fists.
That is the way we stop fights
such as this!"

You had no right to hit me!
I just messed up a game.

I really am sorry.
Can you say the same?

I'm sorry I took away
all of your men.
Can I give you some back?

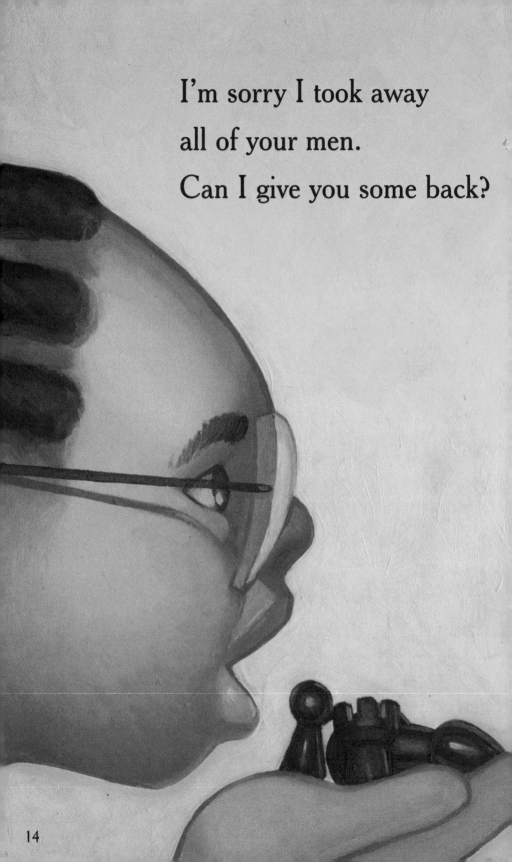

Can we share and play fair?
Can we please
be friends again?

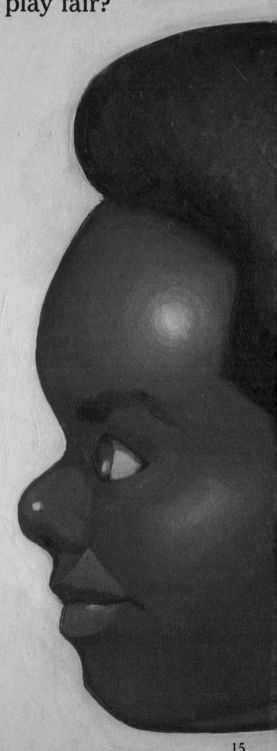

Let's pick up
the broken game.

We can fix it really fast.

We can fix it so it will last.

Let's shake hands.
Let's make up.

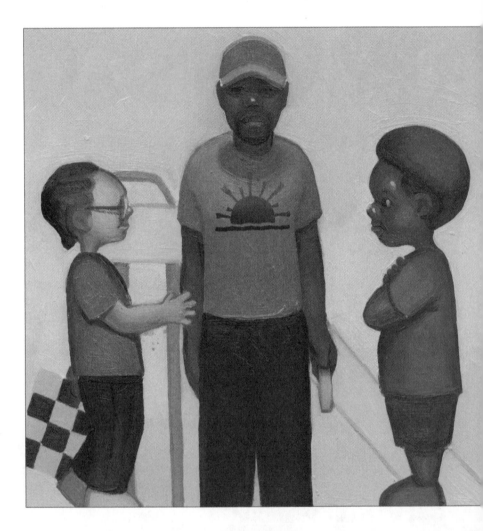

We don't want this fight
to break us up. . . .

You hit me!
Don't hit me!
Don't do that again!
I thought you were my
best friend!

I'm going to hit you back.
You'll see.
I might just kick you!
Do you hear me?

"Use your words!" says Miss Brown.
"Use your words, not your feet.
That is the way we stop fights
on this street."

You're sorry you hit me
again, you say?
You're really sorry?
You still want to play?

You say that you were just
kidding this time?
Let me think about that.
Let me make up my mind.

All right!

Okay!

Here's the deal.

Use your words. . . .

Okay, let's shake hands.
Let's really make up.

▲▲▲▲▲▲ JUST FOR YOU ▲▲▲▲

Here are some things for you to think about.

How Would YOU Feel?

The boy with glasses felt **bad**!
The other boy was **mad**!

Why was he mad?
How would YOU feel?

The boy with glasses
said he was **sorry**!

Why was he sorry?
Would YOU feel sorry?

Then the other boy
said he was sorry!

Why was he sorry?
How would YOU feel?

Now they're both **happy**!
Did a friend ever make
YOU feel happy?

Tell about it.

YOUR Dos and Don'ts

The boys in this story needed help! Miss Brown helped them.

Pretend you have her job. What would YOU tell the boys to **do**? When would you say, **"Don't** do that!"?

▲▲▲TOGETHER TIME ▲▲▲▲

Make some time to share ideas about the story with your young reader! Here are some activities you can try. There are no right or wrong answers.

Talk About It: Even best friends sometimes disagree! Invite your child to talk about a time he or she had an argument with a friend. Ask, "What was the fight about? Did you and your friend 'use your words' to help fix things?"

Think About It: Ask your child, "Which character tells the story? Why do you think the author wrote the story this way? Why do you think she used rhymes?"

Make Your Own Story: Ask your child, "What do you think will happen the next time these two boys play together? Can you make up a story about it?" You can write down the story. Your child can draw pictures to illustrate it.

Act It Out: As you read the story aloud, invite your child to use facial expressions to act out how the narrator (the boy with glasses) feels on each page. When does the boy feel bad? When is he mad? When is he happy?

Meet the Author

Bernette Ford says, "It really bothers me when see boys and girls so quick to hit each other. I wanted to write a fun story to show kids that there are other ways to solve disagreements. One day I heard a teacher in the schoolyard telling two boys, 'Use your words!' That calmed those boys down—and it gave me the idea for this story."

Bernette grew up in Uniondale, New York, and graduated from Connecticut College in New London. She was a children's book editor and publisher in New York City for many years. Now that she works from home as a children's book packager and editorial consultant, she ha more time to do what she likes best—writing children's books! Bernette is married to illustrator George Ford, and they live in Brooklyn, New York. Her first book in the JUST FOR YOU! series, *Hurry Up!*, was published in 2003.

Meet the Artist

Gary Grier says, "Illustrating books is really fun work! You have to get into the characters. The boys I drew in this story came from my imagination. But the more I worked on the paintings, the more they reminded me of friends from my childhood."

Gary grew up in Jacksonville, Florida, and attended art school in Savannah, Georgia, before moving to New York City and graduating from the School of Visual Arts. He was a freelancer for several years, assisting both a noted fine artist and an illustrator, but always working on his own artwork whenever he could. Gary now lives and paints in Savannah. *Don't Hit Me!* is his first children's book.